Nonprofit Quick Guide™

How to Run a Successful Cultivation Event

Linda Lysakowski, ACFRE
Joanne Oppelt, MHA

Nonprofit Quick Guide: How to Run a Successful Cultivation Event

One of the **Nonprofit Quick Guide**™ series

Published by Joanne Oppelt Consulting, LLC

ISBN Print Book: 978-1-951978-07-5

13 12 11 10 9 8 7 6 5 4 3 2 1

About the Authors

LINDA LYSAKOWSKI, ACFRE

Linda is one of approximately one hundred professionals worldwide to hold the Advanced Certified Fundraising Executive designation. Linda is the author of ten nonfiction books, a contributing author, coeditor, or coauthor of eighteen others. She has also written six books in the fiction realm.

Linda has more than thirty years in the development field. She worked for a university and a museum before starting her own consulting firm. In her twenty-seven years as a philanthropic consultant, Linda has managed capital campaigns that have raised more than $50 million, helped hundreds of nonprofit organizations achieve their development goals, and trained more than forty thousand development professionals in most of the fifty states of the United States, Canada, Mexico, Egypt, and Bermuda.

She served on the Association of Fundraising Philanthropy (AFP) Foundation for Philanthropy Board and on the Professional Advancement Division for AFP. She is a past president of the Eastern Pennsylvania and Sierra (Nevada) AFP chapters. She received the Outstanding Fundraiser of the Year award from the Eastern Pennsylvania, Las Vegas, and Sierra (Nevada) chapters of AFP, was honored with the Barbara Marion Award for Outstanding Service to AFP, and received the Lifetime Achievement Award from the Las Vegas AFP chapter.

Linda is a graduate of Alvernia University with majors in banking and finance as well as theology/philosophy, and a minor in communications. As a graduate of AFP's Faculty Training Academy, she is a Master Teacher.

JOANNE OPPELT, MHA

Joanne, principal of Joanne Oppelt Consulting, LLC, is a seasoned rainmaker with a distinguished track record of success. During her twenty-five-plus years working in the nonprofit arena, she built or rebuilt successful fundraising departments at every stop, helping her organizations grow capacity and more effectively fulfill their missions.

She has held positions from grant writer to executive director at the nonprofits Community Access Unlimited, Caring Contact: A Listening Community, Family to Family Network of New Jersey, Christian Healthcare Center, March of Dimes Central New Jersey, Prevent Child Abuse New Jersey, and Maternal and Family Health Services. Her extensive background in a variety of work roles and organizations enables her to understand the realities and challenges nonprofit practitioners face–both internally and externally. Her success at every stop positions her to help any nonprofit, whether through her books or consulting practice, turn around its struggling fundraising operations.

Joanne is the author of four books and coauthor of seven. She has taught at Kean University as an Adjunct Professor in its graduate program. She is also a highly sought-after speaker and presenter.

Joanne holds a master's degree in health administration from Wilkes University, where she graduated with distinction. Her bachelor's degree is in education, with a minor in psychology.

Dedication

This book is dedicated to the staff and volunteers of nonprofits who have learned the secrets of creating relationships before approaching donors for funding. You have taught us a lot.

Contents

Chapter One

What is Cultivation and Why Do You Need It?

What is cultivation?

If you are a gardener, you probably know that you can't just go out and buy a tomato plant, place it on your porch or plant it in your garden, and expect to pick ripe, juicy tomatoes a few weeks later. It takes sunshine, rain (or watering if you live in the desert), fertilizer, pulling off the suckers, and some TLC to be able to reap the rewards of your work at harvest time.

Prospective donors are like plants. They need nurturing to reap the rewards of the harvest— the major gift or big grant. So, you need to understand that cultivating donors is one of the four basic steps of fundraising:

1. Identification
2. Cultivation
3. Solicitation
4. Stewardship

You may not always get to snuggle up to Steve Wozniak, Bill Gates, or Warren Buffet, but developing relationships with your local key business leaders, community leaders, and philanthropists isn't that hard.

For most people, getting in the door is often the hardest part of making an ask. And it is really intimidating for those who have not worked in the business or philanthropic world. How do you get in the door? What do you say if the prospective donor says, "No, we're not interested?" Do you have any relationship with these business and community leaders, or do you have a staff or board member who might? You might be able to cultivate these relationships into stronger ones.

Before we talk about cultivation events, let's talk about the first step in relationship building—identifying who you want to build relationships with.

Identifying prospective donors can start with a series of brainstorming meetings with your board, staff, and development committee. The next steps are the research the prospects' ability to give and the linkage you might have with this person. But let's start with identifying potential prospects. You will probably be surprised to find there might already be some relationships you can nurture. You can use a brainstorming form like this to identify possible connections to potential donors, board members, or volunteers.

Brainstorming Form: Potential Donors/Board Members/ Fundraising Volunteers

Your Name: _____

Category	Name	Potential Major Donor	Potential Board Member	Potential Fundraising Volunteers
My accountant				
My car dealer				
My banker(s)				
My attorney				
Members of my professional association				
My insurance agent				
My doctor(s)				
My dentist(s)				
Members of a service club to which I belong				

Neighbors				
Relatives				
Clients/ customers of mine				
Politicians I know				

People with whom I worship				
People with whom I work				
People with whom I went to school				
Parents of children with whom my children go to school				
My realtor				

People with whom I do business				
People with whom I play sports				
People I know support other charities				
People who have asked me to support their favorite charity				

People I know who volunteer for other nonprofit organizations				
Others				

Once you have a list to start with, you can prioritize the prospective donors you need to cultivate and plan appropriate events for them.

If you struggle with coming up with a list, you can get out there, and get your staff and board members out there, meeting new people.

The first thing you need to do is make sure you are hanging out where the business and community leaders hang out. You won't find them by sitting in your office.

For business leaders, attend a few meetings of your chamber of commerce and see if these leaders are in attendance—even if you do not get to meet them personally. Attend other nonprofit events and see if community leaders attend those events. Ask board members, development committee members, staff members, and other volunteers what they know about these leaders. Do they belong to Rotary or other service clubs? Do they travel a lot for business? Do they have family obligations that keep them at home most evenings, or are they involved in civic groups? You want to find out as much information about them that will help you determine their ability and interests, as well as establish a linkage with them if you don't already have a connection to them.

For community leaders, start with those you have some connection to and see if you can cultivate a stronger relationship. If this leader is a Rotary member, for example, maybe you can arrange to speak to this prospect's Rotary club. If you know a leader is a regular church attender, see if anyone on your board or staff belongs to the same church. If you know the leader attends the symphony, find out which of your board members or staff might also be subscribers to the symphony.

Wrapping It Up

◆ Donor prospects need cultivation just like plants do.

◆ First, you need to try to identify the people you want to cultivate.

◆ Conduct a brainstorming session with your board, your staff, and your development committee.

◆ Prioritize the individuals and groups with whom you want to cultivate a relationship.

Chapter Two

Cultivation Events and Activities—are they different?

Once you have a list of some business and community leaders with whom you have a slight connection, let's see if you can cultivate those relationships into something deeper—before asking them or their companies to support you financially. You can do this through formal cultivation events or through one-on-one visits with these leaders.

The difference between cultivation events and cultivation activities is that activities revolve around building a relationship with one person, while events are used to cultivate groups.

There is a time and place for both.

Activities

One-on-one cultivation activities are used, typically, when you are trying to strengthen an existing relationship. They are also useful when you want feedback of a more intimate nature from the prospective donor, such as trying to better determine the prospect's capability to give or an individual's level of interest in a program. They can even help smooth over a strained relationship.

When meeting with these prospects individually, schedule appointments in the prospects' offices at their convenience. Let them know you will take only thirty to forty minutes of their time. Try to give them as much information as possible in a brief amount of time. Take some leave-behinds, like an annual report, brochure, or fact sheet. But don't expect them to read too much. You might also invite each prospect to take an individual tour of your organization, if appropriate.

Most importantly, however, is *listening* to them for clues about their ability to give and interest in giving.

You are now well on your way to developing a strong relationship with prospective donors.

Events

Donor cultivation events are used when you want to approach a whole new constituency—perhaps medical professionals, attorneys, foundation officers, the media, or business leaders. You want their input but on a more general basis—perhaps ideas for marketing your organization, technology expertise, or fundraising.

Formal cultivation events, such as a Business Leaders' Breakfast, can be a great way to get them more enthused, more involved, and eventually become substantial donors. After these cultivation events, where you identify the key people who will be willing to be volunteers or ambassadors, you can take it to the next level by building more personal relationships with those that express an interest in getting more involved with your organization.

Once you have built strong relationships with community leaders, you want to get them to talk to others about your organization—to serve as "cheerleaders" and "evangelists" for your organization. How do you build those strong relationships? Like any "courtship," it takes time! You start with the identification and cultivation process—the "engagement" process. Once these leaders indicate a desire to get more involved with your organization, you can ask them to serve on a board's committee or a special task force, or just ask their advice on something like marketing, finances, or technology. Eventually, you can invite them to host cultivation events for their colleagues and friends. Or invite them to speak on behalf of your organization or to open the doors to other leaders. After you develop these strong relationships, you will find that these ambassadors from the community will be willing to ask other businesses and community leaders for money. These leaders might even start a "friendly competition" to see who can raise the most money!

Cultivation events are the best place to start when you don't have well-established connections with the people you want to cultivate. It is sort of like "scattering the seed" in the garden. Some seeds will grow and bear fruit; others will get swept away by the wind or fall on barren ground or rocky soil.

The cultivation event is an excellent introduction to your organization. There will undoubtedly be some seeds worth further cultivation by forming a closer, more personal relationship with the people who are really enthused about your organization.

To help you decide what type of cultivation you might want to do with each of the prospects you've identified using the brainstorming form in **Chapter One,** you can prioritize them on a table like this:

Business Leader, Philanthropist, or other Community Leaders	Do We Have Any Relationship with this Leader	To What Groups Does This Leader Belong?	What Are This Leader's Interests	What Type of Cultivation Will be Used
Company (if you have identified business leaders)				

In the "Any Relationship" column, list any possible contacts you might have, even if they are weak connections. You might be able to cultivate them into stronger ones.

In the "To What Groups Does This Leader Belong?" column, you might have to do some research to find this out. You may have spotted them at a chamber of commerce event or some other service or professional group. Ask board members, development committee members, staff members, and other volunteers what they know about these leaders. You might be able to find this information from their friends, relatives, or colleagues. If you meet with the prospect personally, you can start a dialogue and learn more about their interests.

Once you've developed this priority list, you might find some stronger connections with some of these leaders than you thought.

Wrapping It Up

- ◆ Cultivation activities are best used to strengthen existing relationships.
- ◆ Cultivation events are best used to cast a wider net and to cultivate groups of peers.
- ◆ Starting with cultivation events is easier because it is less personal, and you can meet a larger group in a single event.
- ◆ The cultivation event will help you identify those that are really enthused about your organization and may deserve further cultivation.

Chapter Three

What Types of Cultivation Events Can You Do?

The event will depend on the audience.

Individual philanthropists typically are people who have a connection, if not with your organization, with one of your board members, staff members, or volunteers. If you want to cultivate these people, play up that connection. Ask the board member, staff person, or volunteer to host an event in their home, at your organization, or at some other location.

Individual prospects may feel more comfortable in the home of someone they know. You have probably heard of "house parties," "parlor meetings," and the like. So perhaps you can ask your board members to consider inviting their friends and colleagues to a cultivation event once a year. Many board members fear fundraising because they think it is all about asking their friends for money; for them, this is an excellent introduction to fundraising because it does not require them to "make the ask." They will often feel much more comfortable just introducing their friends to your organization, knowing they will not be hit up for money at these events.

For a nonprofit with dedicated development staff, you can think big. If you have twelve board members, and they each host one event a year, that means you will be opening up a new network every month. With twenty-four board members, twice a month! Imagine how many new donors will result from these events. Not only donors, but volunteers, possible board members, and ambassadors who might be willing to host their friends for a similar event once they get to know you better.

If this goal seems overly ambitious for your organization, start small. Plan one or two cultivation events and see how they go. But remember, if your board members are hosting events in their homes, your work is pretty minimal—sending out invitations, handling RSVPs, planning the agenda, and showing up the night of the event. With events held at your organization, there will be more logistics to deal with, so plan accordingly. And remember, you still have all the other functions of development to handle (or, if you are the Executive Director, you still have an organization to run!) However, this is a perfect job for your development committee to tackle; they can be charged with recruiting the hosts and working with them to ensure a successful event. So, you may be able to pull off four cultivation events a year. There is no magic number! Do what works for your organization, but do *something*!

We've seen successful "house party" events held in everything from a small apartment of a board member who hosts six or eight of their friends for a dinner party to a barbeque for 150 people held at a ranch. (We wonder if George Bush and Willie Nelson ever cultivated donors and ambassadors at their ranches!) And everything in between. It can be a cocktail party, a hot dog and hamburger picnic under a tent, or a sit-down dinner. It can be coffee and pastry for breakfast, or a luncheon, or an afternoon tea. The format is dependent on the audience and the host. What will this group be most comfortable with?

Of course, some of your board members may not be comfortable entertaining in their homes. So, they can either team up with another board member or host an event at your organization, a restaurant, their country club, or a neutral location.

Your organization will be a good location if you actually provide services in your building, so they can see your agency in action first-hand. If your services are conducted out in the community, it will be a little harder to demonstrate your success, but there are ways around that. One event that Linda helped organize was for an organization that served people with disabilities. Their services were provided in the form of residential housing all over the county and social activities throughout the community. So instead of organizing an event at their organization, they had a business leaders' breakfast in a local restaurant, and they gave attendees a "virtual tour" of the organization through a PowerPoint presentation. They had photographed residents in their group homes—with their permission, of course—and different social activities in which residents participated. It was a great way to introduce the organization and its value to the community.

We find that many times the events that most organizations tend to shy away from are the events for business leaders, even though this is a group most nonprofits really need to cultivate. This is a market many nonprofits don't feel comfortable with because they don't know how to relate to business leaders. They are far more comfortable in the nonprofit atmosphere. Here's where your board or development committee can help. They may have relationships with business leaders they can capitalize on. Put those board members or development committee members with strong business connections in charge of these events.

A Primo Cultivation Idea: Business Leaders' Breakfast

Business leaders are a tough audience for some of the types of events we've mentioned above. They are busy people and usually don't want to attend a lunch meeting. It takes them out of their office in the middle of the workday. And often, they can't get out of their office to attend a "happy hour" event. Although if you are really narrowing your audience to a specific field, this might change the format. A group of attorneys, for example, may be free only after the courts close, so maybe a happy hour at a cigar bar is appropriate for them. Stockbrokers are often at work in the early morning when the international market trade is busy, so the best time for them may also be after hours. On the other hand, if your audience is media people, they usually have late afternoon deadlines, or maybe an appearance on the five o'clock news, so morning is the only time you might be able to get them to attend.

Business leaders generally will attend early-morning meetings before they go to the office. So, plan cultivation events for the general business community in the morning and don't keep them too long. We'll talk more about this in a future chapter, but it will be critical that you let invitees know the time commitment. Generally, a meeting that goes longer than an hour and fifteen minutes gives them a good excuse to say, "No, I can't commit to that much time away from the office."

A critical step in the planning process for your event is to identify your audience. We will talk more about that in the next chapter. We'll also talk about planning your event in the next few chapters. Another important step is to find a person to chair the event—which we'll cover in **Chapter Five.** Then you will plan your agenda, which is covered in **Chapter Six.**

Wrapping It Up:

- ◆ The most important thing to keep in mind when planning your event is your audience.
- ◆ The host of your event will also play a big role in choosing the right event.

◆ There are numerous types of events that will work for each audience.

◆ Business leaders most often like early morning events, but again, know your audience.

Chapter Four

Who Hosts Cultivation Events

The host is one of the critical factors of a successful event. Do not send out an invitation signed by the executive director! It might sound weird, but it gives the impression that you don't have community support. And, consider how many of your invitees will even recognize your executive director's name. As we said, individual philanthropists will be more comfortable if they are invited to a friend's home, or to your organization, or a neutral location, if their friend is hosting the event.

If you're holding a cultivation event for media, a well-known and respected media leader makes the best host. If you plan a cultivation event for clergy, choose a well-respected member of the clergy to host your event. If foundation leaders are your target audience, perhaps the head of a large foundation would be a good host. For business cultivation events, select a well-known business leader who will be known and respected by the list of leaders you want to invite to the event. If you don't already have these relationships, some good places to start:

◆ Go back to the brainstorming sessions you've done with the board, staff, and volunteers. You will probably be surprised to find that board members, staff members, and volunteers have some interesting connections.

◆ Talk to some of your vendors who have a vested interest in your organization's success.

Occasionally a well-respected political leader may be a good host, but usually, this is advised against because it can be a polarizing factor. Although some political leaders are respected by most parties, this is becoming rare in today's society. The same can be said about celebrities. Even if you have access to celebrities, they can fall out of favor if there is unfavorable publicity surrounding them.

No host will be "liked by everybody," but try to choose someone who is not too controversial and, most importantly, will be respected by your audience.

Linda recalls working with an environmental group that secured Robert Kennedy Jr. to chair a campaign. While not particularly popular in some circles, he was perfect for this event because of his work to preserve the environment. Another client struggled with asking one of its state's United States Senators because she was considered controversial in some circles, although she was passionate about their cause.

Preferably the person selected to host your event will already be familiar with and have a passion for your organization. It could be a board member, a member of your development committee, a major donor, a volunteer, or someone connected to one of your board or staff members (perhaps an employer).

You can use a list like this to help brainstorm for the right host. Adapt it to your audience if it is not a business leader's event.

Suggestions for Business Leader Breakfast Event

Name	Title	Business	Contact Info	Who in Our Organization Can Ask This Leader to Chair the Event?

Now, prioritize the list. Who is the best person to chair the event? Second best? And so on?

Choose several dates that will work for your organization before approaching the first person on your list. When you contact this person, be sure to mention why you want them to chair the event and the event's purpose. Make it clear that you are not asking for money but for advice from those who attend this event.

Once you have a chair, let this person know you will write a letter of invitation. If the chair is willing to use their company or personal letterhead and envelopes, that will look more personal than using your organization's letterhead, and it will attract the attention of the invitees. You should accept the RSVPs at your office, though. Do not expect the chair to handle this. Share your list of invitees with the chair, and make sure everyone on the list is approved by the chair. Also, ask the chair if there are any names you should add to your list.

You will also want to share the agenda and all the materials you'll be using at the event with the host and ask for their input on that, as well. You don't want surprises for your host. Have the host participate in developing the agenda, give them talking points to cover in their welcoming address, and any other role they may be playing, such as leading the open discussion period.

Wrapping It Up

- ◆ The host is one of the most critical success factors in a cultivation event.
- ◆ Choose the host based on your audience; it must be someone they know and respect.
- ◆ Do not have your executive director host your cultivation events!
- ◆ Make it easy for your host to say, "yes."

Chapter Five

Who Gets Invited and How

So, now you have your host. The next step is to develop your invitation list and run it by the host. This is very important. If there is someone on your list that the host does not feel comfortable with, invite them to another event with a different host. You don't want the host or any guests to feel uncomfortable. Also, the host may have ideas for friends or colleagues they want to add to your list.

Who should you invite? In most cases, your invitees will have some knowledge of your organization. Members, donors, clients, former clients, volunteers, people on your newsletter mailing list, and others you want to cultivate into a deeper relationship. If you have recently moved, you may want to invite your new neighbors, businesses, or individuals. If you are trying to cultivate collaboration, you may even want to invite other nonprofit leaders.

If you seek government funding or support of any kind, you will want to invite elected and appointed government officials to your event.

If you are trying to increase awareness, invite media representatives.

Perhaps you seek support from a specific audience, for example, teachers, healthcare professionals, members of the clergy, attorneys, or marketing professionals.

Start by developing a preliminary list.

Cultivation Event(s) Invitation List

Business or Community Leader	Title	Company	Address	Phone	Gate-keeper (If Available)	Email (If Available)

If your list is long or too diverse, you will want to plan several events. Sometimes organizations organize business or community invitees by category—bankers and financial people, utility company leaders, high-tech company leaders, insurance company executives, etc.

You will probably want to invite about twenty-five to fifty leaders to each event. You should try for a number of attendees of between ten and twenty for most events, but remember, not everyone you invite will be able to attend. Do not take this as a total lack of interest. It may just be bad timing, so keep these people on your list unless they indicate they are not at all interested.

The invitation itself is important. Keep it short—a one-page letter is the best option, signed by the host and on his or her letterhead if possible. You will get more people to open the letter if it arrives with an important-looking envelope and the letter is signed by someone they know and respect. If the host does not feel comfortable with this, you can use your letterhead and have them sign it, but it will be more effective if it comes directly from the host.

Be sure you tell them the location and the time, and, especially with busy people, let them know how long the event will last. And, most critically, tell them they are not going to be asked for money.

Give them an easy way to respond-an email or text option in addition to a phone number. The responses should be received and tracked by your organization but report back to the host the status of responses. You may also want to plan follow up calls from people you haven't heard from by the RSVP date.

Example

Following is an example of a letter of invitation:

Date
Name
Title
Company
Address
City, State Zip

Dear (NAME):

I would like you to join me for a breakfast get-together on mm/dd/yy from 7:30 a.m. to 8:30 a.m., at XYZ, address.

As a long-time supporter of XYZ, I am delighted to sponsor this breakfast to introduce new friends to XYZ and the tremendously important work they are doing in our community.

You will be treated to a continental breakfast, a brief tour of the XYZ facility, and will be asked to participate in a short discussion that will help XYZ's strategic planning process. The breakfast will end by 8:30 a.m. Let me assure you that this is NOT A SOLICITATION FOR FUNDS.

Please respond by calling CONTACT at (XXX) XXX-XXXX or emailing Email.com by mm/dd/yyyy so we can plan accordingly. I know you will enjoy, along with other community leaders, hearing more about XYZ Organization and providing them with your expert advice. If you have any questions, please feel free to call me at (XXX) XXX-XXXX. I look forward to seeing you on mm/dd/yyyy.

Sincerely,

HOST

Wrapping It Up

- ◆ Develop your invitation list and segment it if necessary.
- ◆ Don't forget to review the list with the host.
- ◆ If possible, ask the host to send the letter on his or her letterhead.
- ◆ Be sure to tell the invitees that this is not an "ask event."
- ◆ Track responses and plan on follow up calls if needed.
- ◆ Make it easy for the invitees to respond and track responses.

Chapter Six

Planning the Agenda

U nless your event is a dinner party, plan a light meal, and keep your agenda brief, especially if you are hosting business leaders and others who have a limited time frame.

A suggested agenda would include the following:

- ◆ A brief welcome from the host
- ◆ A brief update from your CEO explaining your programs and how you are addressing community needs
- ◆ A tour or virtual tour of your organization or a testimonial
- ◆ Time for questions and "advice-giving."

The host must take the lead role in the event. Make it clear at the recruiting stage that the host is expected to welcome the guests and give brief but inspiring opening remarks. This is why the host must have some relationship with your organization. If their experience is limited, invite the host in for a tour and meeting with your executive director so they will be enthused and inspired before they are expected to inspire others. Be sure to answer any questions the host may have before the event. Provide them with information such as your strategic plan, your annual report, and anything else they have questions about. You also want to make sure when you are selecting your host that they are already seen as an inspiring leader and can motivate your guests.

Next, your CEO should briefly describe your organization, its programs, and your outcomes—how you are changing and/or saving lives. And your plans for the future. If your CEO is not an enthusiastic, inspiring presenter, ask them if they would like you to prepare talking points for the presentation and rehearse the presentation with them. You can prepare remarks in advance or give them talking points to work from. You may want to have some other key staff present, especially those in charge of programs, to answer questions the guests may have and to speak with enthusiasm about the difference you make in the community.

After these presentations, you can give guests a hands-on experience with your nonprofit. A virtual tour, like the one we talked about in **Chapter Four,** or, better yet, a live tour if there is activity going on in your facility. Another cool idea is to have some testimonials from users of your services. This is the most effective way to put a face on your programs—to have them hear from someone whose life was changed or saved by your organization.

Be sure to allow plenty of time for questions and discussion. Getting feedback from guests is the most critical outcome for these events. For example, you may want to allow time for guests to complete a brief questionnaire. We will cover that in a future chapter. Here is a sample agenda:

XYZ Organization
Community Leaders' Breakfast

Agenda

7:30 Continental Breakfast

7:45 Welcome..Host

7:50 An Introduction to XYZ .... Executive Director

8:00 Questions & Answers.. All

8:15 Completion of Questionnaire .... Guests

8:20 Tour of Facility

Wrapping It Up

◆ Keep your agenda short.
◆ Make sure the host is familiar enough with your organization to speak passionately about it.
◆ Prepare staff for their presentation by providing a script or talking points, but make sure they are not just reading a script.
◆ Allow plenty of time for feedback and questions; listening is critical.

Chapter Seven

Telling Your Story

Here are some examples of successful cultivation events and how they told their stories. These are good examples of telling your story by putting a face on it. See if something like this will work for your organization.

Example One

A local emergency shelter wanted to embark on an annual corporate appeal; however, most of the community really didn't understand the organization's full range of services. One of the board members, the president of a local bank, agreed to talk to the CEO of a large manufacturing firm in the city. This CEO agreed to host a cultivation event for local business leaders to become more familiar with the shelter and its mission. He agreed to review the suggested invitation list and added a few names to the list. While preparing for the event, we invited the host to take a tour himself. The more involved he became with the shelter, the more enthused he became. He agreed to send out the invitation letter on his letterhead and said his office would even handle printing and mailing the letters that the development office had written. The letter clearly stated that this was not a fundraising event and that the attendees would not be asked to contribute that day. We had anticipated that inviting seventy-five business leaders would result in about twenty attending. Due to the perceived importance of the invitation from the host, we were delighted that we had close to sixty business leaders attend that morning.

The event was a 7:30 a.m. breakfast, and the invitation clearly stated that we would end by 8:45 a.m. The host first welcomed guests. He told them how impressed he had been as he learned more about the shelter's many services. He explained that the services included much more than providing a bed for the night but extended to daycare for homeless children, training in resume and job interview skills, medical and dental clinics, and more. The shelter director then thanked everyone for coming, gave a brief history of the shelter, expanded on the number of people served, and told the group how the shelter was funded. The participants all understood the work of the shelter much better after this informal breakfast meeting.

The piece d 'resistance was a tour of the shelter led by a former shelter guest, who showed the business leaders around the shelter, pointing out, "I used to sleep in that bed in the corner. Now I have a job at the shelter, my own apartment, and am getting my life together." Several of the business leaders attending were so moved by this experience, they wanted to write out a check on the spot. However, the organization said, "No, we told you we would not ask for money at this event, and we are very serious about our promise. But, rest assured, we will be contacting you at a later time!"

When these business leaders were later approached for the annual appeal, they responded very generously because they now had a deep personal connection to the organization. At least a dozen of those who had attended the event volunteered to speak to other business leaders about their commitment to the shelter, as well.

Example Two

Another homeless shelter held a fantastic cultivation event for the mid-level manager of a large bank in their community. They targeted one company at a time for which they would host an event. At this particular event, as with others they held, the business leaders were invited to breakfast with the shelter guests. They sat at the same tables and shared a meal with the shelter guests. After breakfast, the executive director took the business leaders on a brief tour and showed them first-hand the need for more space. But the thing that stuck in the minds of these potential funders was that they had shared a meal with someone who needed their help.

Example Three

A free medical clinic wanted to tell its story to local medical professionals and philanthropists, who they invited to tour the clinic. One of the issues they dealt with is what many agencies like free clinics, homeless shelters, and drug and alcohol clinics face. The "these people deserve the situations they are in now, so why we should help them?" This agency got video testimonials from some of the people they helped. One was from an RN who suddenly found herself uninsured because of a change in her position. After hearing her story, attendees thought, "Wow, this could happen to anyone—

maybe even me or someone I love." This changed their attitude about the type of clientele served by the clinic and resulted in building relationships, which led to future donations, including some major gifts.

There are many ways to tell your story at these events. Consider what might work best for *your* organization.

Example Four

A human service agency that had developed its first-ever case for support wanted to test the case to see if it would be compelling to the local business community. The development committee chair invited several business leaders to come to the agency for a luncheon to which he treated the guests. After lunch, the host welcomed people and explained that they would not be asked for money, as indicated in the letter of invitation, but simply for advice. The executive director talked briefly about the organization's history and needs, and the development director presented the case for support that had been put into a PowerPoint format. After viewing the presentation, the host asked the guests what they thought of the case: "Were there parts that seemed more urgent than others? Was there anything they would eliminate or add? How did they think the case should be presented to businesses?" And the final question, "If you were asked to contribute to this organization, would this case prompt you to make a gift?"

The organization gained some valuable input from these business leaders. It saved a lot of money by not printing something that might not tell an accurate story or be compelling enough to prompt a gift.

Example Five

A drug and alcohol counseling center wanted to involve business leaders in its work. This group planned a breakfast for business and political leaders in its community. About seventy people attended. As with the shelter mentioned above, they had a businessperson host the event and welcome the guests. Then they asked the executive director to talk about the agency. They had two persons who gave brief testimonials. One was a judge who spoke about how much money this organization saved taxpayers because it provided services that kept people out of the court system and helped them build new lives. She made quite an impressive presentation on the rational side of the case. As in the case of the shelter, this organization had an employee who had been a former client of the center, and she gave a vivid testimonial about how the agency had helped change her life. Again, an emotional and rational appeal helped present the agency's case to the business community.

At the end of the breakfast, brief questionnaires were distributed, asking how the organization might partner with the companies represented. When the questionnaires were collected and reviewed, the organization had found a volunteer to design the agency newsletter, a company that agreed to print and mail the newsletter for them, and several people who indicated they would be interested in serving on the development committee to help the organization raise funds.

Example Six

A museum seeking government funding from national, state, and local sources, held a series of lectures to which they invited government officials and staff members to attend the lectures followed by receptions where they got to meet the speakers up close and personal. These receptions allowed the government officials to look at the type of critical programming the museum was running and enlist their support for government grants and appropriations.

Wrapping It Up

- ◆ You can best tell your story by putting a human face on it.
- ◆ You can use testimonials, videos, PowerPoint presentations, or tours of your facility to help tell your story.
- ◆ Base your message on your audience. Businesspeople like to hear that you are helping people become independent, that you are saving tax dollars, and that you have a plan.
- ◆ Next to listening to your attendees, telling your story well is the most important part of the event.

Chapter 8

Listening to Your Audience

L isten, listen, listen. As we have said in other books in the Nonprofit Quick Guide™ series, humans have two ears and one mouth for a really good reason. We should spend twice as much time listening as we do talking. So, if you haven't gotten the message yet, this is the most critical part of cultivation events. Allow plenty of time for discussion, and listen, listen, listen. Have someone take notes of the discussion.

You will want to first ask if your guests have any questions about your presentation and storytelling. If they have taken a tour as part of your storytelling, have them gather after the tour for a debriefing.

When it comes to the open-discussion part, have someone facilitate the discussion, usually the event host. Questions you might consider include:

- ◆ Are there community needs you think our organization should be addressing?
- ◆ Are there ways you think we can better market our programs to the community?
- ◆ For businesses, do you have an employee volunteer program? If so, would your employees be interested in volunteering in any way for us?
- ◆ What other advice do you have for us?

You can also design a brief—repeat after me, "brief"—questionnaire that you ask participants to fill out and turn in when they leave. This can be used for more specific answers, such as, "who else do you recommend we invite to future cultivation events?" Make sure you have a staff person to collect their responses.

An example follows:

XYZ Organization
Community Leaders' Breakfast

Questionnaire

1. Before today, were you acquainted with XYZ? If so, what did you know about us?

_____

_____

_____

_____

_____

_____

2. List other colleagues you would suggest we invite to future events?

_____

_____

_____

_____

_____

_____

3. Are there ways we could partner with your company/organization to better serve our community?

_____

_____

_____

_____

_____

_____

4. Would you be willing to become more involved with XYZ? If yes, in what capacity?

_____

_____

_____

_____

_____

_____

Often this dialogue will give you some important suggestions. Make sure participants know you intend to follow up on their suggestions. And tell them you will contact them if you need clarification on any of their responses.

Wrapping It Up

◆ Listening to participants is the most important part of a cultivation event.

◆ Allow time for open discussion.

◆ Be sure to take notes.

◆ Give them a brief questionnaire to respond to more specific questions.

Chapter Nine

Follow Up

O nce you've held your cultivation event(s), the next step is following up with attendees, particularly those who asked for more information or suggested possible partnership arrangements or employee volunteering opportunities. Do the follow-up one-on-one with the person who attended the event.

Track your follow-up information on a list, which will then be added to your database.

Follow-Up from Cultivation Event

Date of event: _____

Event host: _____

Attendee	Contact Info	Questions Requiring Follow-Up	Possible Volunteer Opportunity	Possible Funding Opportunity	Other

You will also want to follow up with those who did not attend the event. Make a list of those who did not attend.

Follow up to Non-Attendees

Date of event: _____

Event host: _____

Invitee	Reason for Not Attending (If Known)	Invite to Future Event	Remove from List	Cultivate Individually

If many people simply did not find your first date or time convenient, you will probably want to hold a second event to accommodate them. Some of the people invited might not find any of your times convenient and might need to be contacted individually. Make a list of those you want to contact individually.

Individual Cultivation Prospects Follow Up

Name	Company	Contact Information	Gatekeeper (If Known)	The person from Our Organization Who Should Schedule Appointment

When meeting with these prospects individually, schedule appointments in the prospects' offices at their convenience. Let them know you will take only thirty to forty minutes of their time. Since you can't conduct a real-live tour at these meetings, try to give them as much information as possible in a brief amount of time. Take some leave-behinds, like an annual report, brochure, or fact sheet. But don't expect them to read too much.

For discussion purposes, you can use the same questions used during the cultivation event. You don't want to be taking copious notes during the meeting, but as soon as you get outside the office, jot down any important notes—especially if there is any follow-up information you need to provide for each prospect. You might also invite each prospect to take an individual tour of your organization if that is appropriate.

You will also want to call everyone who filled out a questionnaire at the event. You can thank them and ask about any of their responses that might need clarification. Ask how they enjoyed the event and if there is additional information they would like to receive.

Questionnaire Response Follow Up

Name	Company	Answers	Clarification on responses	Requested Follow Up Information

With this follow up process, you are now well on your way to developing strong relationships with business and community leaders, such as media personalities, government officials and staff, philanthropists, or specialty audiences you want to cultivate.

You might try a few other tactics, such as asking your board members to host events in their homes if they are on friendly terms with the leaders you want to cultivate. However, many businesspeople would rather keep these types of activities to work hours. And, spouses might not be interested in hearing about something they perceive as business-related activities. But these "house party" events are great for individual philanthropists who feel comfortable in the home of a host with whom they socialize.

Wrapping It Up

◆ Follow up with event attendees and thank them for attending.

◆ Follow up with non-attendees, see if they are interested in attending a future event.

◆ Be sure to provide any additional information requested.

◆ Keep track of all responses in your database.

Chapter Ten

Bringing It All Together

We've tried to cover every aspect of your cultivation event, from securing the host and deciding who should be invented, to the invitation letters and the agenda, to storytelling, and, most importantly, listening.

We believe if you follow this formula, you will run successful cultivation events that lead to major gifts for your organization.

1. Select the audience(s) you want to cultivate
2. Choose the best host for this audience
3. Select an appropriate venue
4. Send the invitation, clearly stating that this is not a fundraising event
5. Track responses and follow up if necessary
6. Coach all participants on the agenda and their role
7. Tell your story emotionally and rationally
8. Listen to your audience
9. Follow up with attendees and those who did not attend
10. Evaluate your success and plan your next event(s)

However, don't get intimated by the process. It is actually quite simple. You'll find after you do one event, it gets easier.

Set lofty goals, but don't try to do it all overnight. Start with three or four events a year, if that is all you feel your organization can tackle. Be sure you involve your board and other volunteers in this process. This is a good project for your development committee to tackle. And remember, this is a perfect project for reluctant board members who have a fear of asking for gifts. They don't have to ask because there is no asking at these events.

If you have a tight budget, perhaps board members, the hosts, or sponsors can pick up the tab for your events.

So, put on your gardening gloves and start cultivating. You will be reaping the harvest soon.

www.ingramcontent.com/pod-product-compliance
Lightning Source LLC
Chambersburg PA
CBHW071522210326
41597CB00018B/2855